T0048241

ROCK'N'ROLL PIANO

THE COMPLETE GUIDE WITH AUDIO!

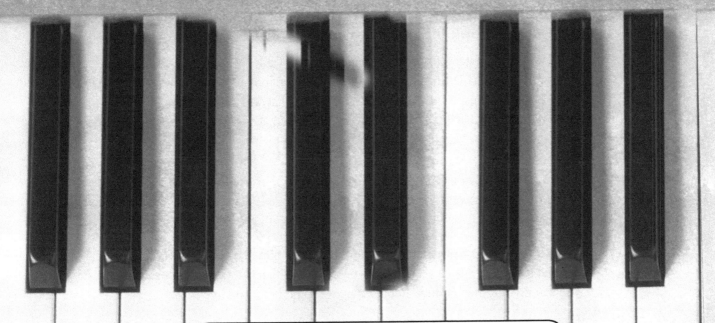

To access audio visit:
www.halleonard.com/mylibrary

8816-6894-3570-9281

BY ANDY VINTER

With additional musical input by
Martin Smith

ISBN 978-0-634-05046-X

HAL•LEONARD®
CORPORATION

7777 W. BLUEMOUND RD. P.O. BOX 13819 MILWAUKEE, WI 53213

Visit Hal Leonard Online at www.halleonard.com

INTRODUCTION

Welcome to the world of early rock 'n' roll piano! This book will teach you the basic skills you'll need to take your place alongside Fats Domino, Jerry Lee Lewis, Little Richard, and the other great rock 'n' roll piano players of the fifties and sixties.

Rock 'n' Roll Piano is divided into three sections. Before you get started, here's the lowdown on what you can expect:

Part 1: What Is Rock 'n' Roll?

This first section aims to put rock 'n' roll in the context of fifties and early sixties music. Throughout, you'll find explanations of the popular music styles of the time, influential artists, producers, and record labels. Investigate some of the suggested listening, and really immerse yourself in the world of rock 'n' roll. (If you want more info, check out some of the Internet resources listed at the end of the chapter.)

Part 2: Rock 'n' Roll Piano Techniques

This next section gets down to the nitty gritty of how to play rock 'n' roll piano. You'll learn all the essential left-hand patterns, chord progressions, and specialized right-hand techniques—glissandos, crushed notes, note clusters, etc.—that will get you sounding like a true rock 'n' roller. We'll also discuss how to practice, as well as the basics of how to solo in rock 'n' roll.

Part 3: Style File

In this last section, you'll find six complete rock 'n' roll tunes in different styles. By this point, you'll have learned all the skills, techniques, and tricks you need to be able to play each of these tunes—so go for it. Start "ripping it up"!

This book assumes that you are already familiar with the basics of piano, that you can read music without too much difficulty, and that you can play "hands together" to a reasonable standard. If you can do this, then nothing in these pages should be beyond you.

If at any point you start to feel disheartened or discouraged, remember that many of the great rock 'n' roll pianists were self-taught. They came up with their own techniques and individual styles to suit their particular way of playing, and you can do the same. If you find certain techniques difficult or awkward, then you don't have to use them—that's the beauty of rock 'n' roll!

About the Audio

You'll find audio demonstrations of all the examples as well as backing tracks that you can play along with. First listen to the demo track to hear your part and how it fits in with the whole band, then play along with the backing track (full band, minus piano) when you're ready. Some examples also have slow and fast (full-speed) versions. All tracks have a one-bar count-in.

Piano, keyboard, and organ: Andy Vinter
Guitar, bass, and drums: Martin Smith
Saxophone: Martin Williams
Trumpet: Mark White

CONTENTS

Part One

WHAT IS ROCK 'N' ROLL?

Rock 'n' roll exploded onto America's music scene in the mid fifties—but where did it come from? Well, like other forms of popular music, rock 'n' roll was an amalgamation of many other music styles; it took elements from the blues, boogie woogie, country and western, gospel, and others, and combined them in a way that was entirely new. The power of this new and potent musical force, together with the contemporary changes in American society in the early fifties, proved unstoppable!

The title of "first rock 'n' roll record" is a hotly disputed one. Howlin' Wolf and Ike Turner have a claim with their 1951 recording "Rocket 88." Others cite the recording made on Monday, July 5th, 1954 by guitarist Scotty Moore and fledgling vocalist Elvis Presley of the old blues tune "That's All Right Mama" by Arthur "Big Boy" Crudup.

Whoever claims the title, there is no doubt that the Southern states were the crucible in which rock 'n' roll was forged. The fertile musical cultures of Georgia, Mississippi, Tennessee, and the other states of the deep South created an environment in which musicians were able to blend elements of country music, boogie woogie, gospel, and R&B. As itinerant black musicians moved from city to city, they were exposed to different styles and instrumentations; blues guitarists heard Creole music in New Orleans, and white country musicians heard R&B bands.

The invention of the electric guitar in 1948 (the first commercially available solid-bodied model was Leo Fender's "Broadcaster," later renamed the "Telecaster") allowed urban musicians to make themselves heard in crowded clubs and bars, and their music became harder and more rhythmic. Meanwhile, the spread of radio, TV, and jukeboxes made it even easier for young music fans to hear new music—and crucially, for white kids to hear black music. For it was when the melodic sensibility of white country and western was grafted to the raw sexuality of black R&B that the essence of rock 'n' roll was created—and this was a sound that young white America was desperate to hear.

The Teenager and Fifties Culture

It wasn't until the fifties that teenagers were recognized as a distinct demographic group within society—until that point, the years of puberty and rebellion between childhood and adulthood simply did not have a name. With wartime rationing at an end, and full-time employment and general prosperity becoming the norm following WWII, fifties teenagers found themselves with money to spare and none of the worries that their parents had grown up with. They were free to devote their time and attention to the things that really mattered—clothes, hairstyles, cars... and the opposite sex!

The common musical genres of the era were country music, gospel, jazz, jump, R&B, and pop. Pop music at the beginning of the fifties was the dominant musical force, and probably the only (non-classical) music listened to by middle and upper class white families. Produced by a small number of major record companies, songs were written by Tin Pan Alley songwriters and matched to artists by record company executives. The artist frequently had no input into which songs they sang, or the arrangement and presentation of the songs that they were offered.

Teenagers' obsessions were not reflected by this type of music—songs were generally innocent and featured feather-light melodies, inoffensive lyrics, and wholesome singers like Pat Boone, Rosemary Clooney, and Perry Como. Black "race records" were much more risqué, and even referred to sex euphemistically ("rock and roll" was used as a term for sex as far back as the twenties), but for most white teenagers it was unthinkable that they would listen to them.

America in the early fifties was a still deeply divided country—Rosa Parks hadn't yet demanded her seat on the bus, and segregated schools were still legal. Negro music was simultaneously threatening and appealing to rebellious white teenagers, and young music fans in the early fifties sought it out eagerly. "Sixty Minute Man," recorded in 1951 by the Dominoes, was the first significant R&B record to sell in large quantities to white teenagers, with its heavy beat and suggestive lyrics repelling parents and attracting their children in equal measure.

TV, Radio, and the Jukebox

Teenagers also had access to radios and television, and disc jockeys and radio stations were crucial in the spreading popularity of rock 'n' roll (indeed, it was Cleveland DJ Alan Freed who dubbed the new music "rock and roll"). Transistor radios become smaller and more affordable, and sound quality improved. At the same time, parents began replacing their first televisions with newer models, and their teenage children were often given the old one. Programs hosted by personality DJs began to feature rhythm and blues and doo-wop.

The development of the jukebox was another catalyst that allowed teenagers to hear music that they had never been exposed to before. After a halt in production from 1942, ordered by the US government to conserve materials and labor for the war effort, production resumed in 1946. Crucially, people listening to the newly invented 45s on the jukebox had no idea whether the singer was black or white—black kids thought Bill Black, Carl Perkins, and Steve Cropper were Negroes singing, while white patrons heard, and grew to love, black artists.

Dancing was another teenage obsession that helped to fuel the rock 'n' roll craze. Fast dances based on wartime favorites like the Lindy and Jitterbug allowed youngsters to get energy out of their system and demonstrate their athletic prowess. Slow ballads (often in 12/8) were included to allow the less coordinated teens to join in.

The development of early rock 'n' roll is best understood by examining the musical backgrounds and careers of some of its major stars, nearly all of whom came to prominence in a golden period from 1954-58.

Rock 'n' Roll Heroes

Bill Haley

Bill Haley was born in Highland Park, Michigan on July 6th, 1925. He made his first record at the age of 18 ("Candy Kisses") and spent his early twenties playing as a guitarist in country and western bands like the Downhomers, The Four Aces of Western Swing, and the Saddlemen. However, in 1952, Bill decided that a new and exciting sound was required, and he changed the name of his band to Bill Haley & The Comets. Bill and the band began to reap the rewards of their name and style change almost immediately, as their track "Rock the Joint" sold 75,000 copies.

In 1954, after signing a deal with Decca Records, Bill released a track called "Rock Around the Clock," which had originally been recorded by Sunny Dae in 1952. With sales topping 75,000, the song was a modest hit, but when, twelve months later, the song was used as the title track of *The Blackboard Jungle,* a movie about juvenile delinquents, it exploded, becoming the first record to really introduce rock 'n' roll to America's white teenagers.

His next two records, "Shake, Rattle and Roll" and "See You Later, Alligator," both went on to sell over a million copies. However, Bill's popularity began to fade after 1955, as he was compared unfavorably with the new crop of younger and more energetic rock and rollers like Little Richard, Jerry Lee Lewis, and Elvis Presley.

Elvis Presley

Elvis is, for many people, the embodiment of rock 'n' roll—a teen idol who combined white and black influences and become *the* popular cultural icon of the twentieth century. His overtly sexual stage presence and smoldering good looks, coupled with the driving rhythmic force of his records, ensured a meteoric rise to fame throughout 1955-56.

Elvis was born on January 8th, 1935, in East Tupelo, Mississippi. He first showed musical talent at the age of 10, when he placed second in a talent contest at the Alabama Fair and Dairy Show (singing "Old Shep") and soon after took up the guitar.

However, it wasn't until after he graduated from high school that he cut his first record. Local entrepreneur Sam Phillips operated a scheme where anyone could record a ten-inch acetate for four dollars, and it was at his Memphis Recording Studios that the 18-year old Elvis recorded "My Happiness" and "That's When Your Heartaches Begin."

Following appearances on local radio and TV shows, Elvis enjoyed regional success in Spring 1955 with "Good Rockin' Tonight," but at this stage he was still considered a country act. However, something was obviously happening because his May 13th appearance in Jacksonville started a riot, and in July his recording of "Baby Let's Play House" reached #10 on the national country-and-western chart.

Influential styles

Boogie Woogie

Highly percussive piano style that emerged in the late twenties. Characterized by repetitive left-hand patterns teamed with improvisation in the right hand. Developed in Kansas City by pianists like Pete Johnson and Joe Turner. The term came from "booger-rooger," meaning a swinging party, used by Texas bluesman Blind Lemon Johnson.

Suggested listening:

Jimmy Yancy	*In The Beginning*
Meade Lux Lewis	*The Blues Piano Artistry of Meade Lux Lewis*
Albert Ammons/Meade Lux Lewis	*The First Day*
Pete Johnson	*Central Avenue Boogie*

In September 1955, Elvis had his first #1 country record ("Mystery Train") and, after signing a deal with RCA records, made his national TV debut in January 1956 on the Dorsey brothers' *Stage Show*. Elvis was now a national star and a household name. Later in the year, his first film, *Love Me Tender,* was released, and recouped its $1 million production cost in three days. Throughout 1956, Elvis released a selection of singles that are now regarded as rock 'n' roll classics, including "Heartbreak Hotel," "Blue Suede Shoes," "Hound Dog," "Love Me Tender," and "Don't Be Cruel."

During this period, Elvis's swiveling stage antics continued to provoke outrage, with teachers, clergymen, and other performers claiming that his style was too suggestive. On one appearance on the *Ed Sullivan Show,* he was shown only from the waist up, for fear that his gyrating hips might offend viewers.

Elvis's success continued on an unprecedented scale. In February 1957, "All Shook Up" stayed at #1 for eighteen weeks, and he enjoyed further hits in the same year with "Teddy Bear" and "Jailhouse Rock." Even a draft notice couldn't stop Elvis—his manager Colonel Parker ensured that a steady supply of singles (recorded before his departure) were released after Elvis entered the military. Despite joining the U.S. Army in March 1958, Elvis still managed to earn over $2 million in that year!

Jerry Lee Lewis

In 1955, as Elvis's fame grew, other aspiring rock and rollers made their way to Memphis to seek out his producer, Sam Phillips. Among other future stars like Carl Perkins and Roy Orbison was the son of a Louisiana farmer, Jerry Lee Lewis. Legend has it that Jerry sold all the eggs on his father's farm to pay for his trip to Memphis, and that he then camped out on Phillips's doorstep until he got an audition. However, once inside, he failed to impress Sam and was told to go away and "learn some rock and roll"; three weeks later, he was back, hammering away at the piano in his trademark style.

His first record with Sam's label, Sun Records, was a cover of the country song "Crazy Arms," originally recorded by Ray Price. However, it was with his second single, "Whole Lotta Shakin' Goin' On'," released in 1957, that he really hit the big time. Initially banned as obscene, his manic, piano-wrecking style was a huge hit across America, and the single went on to top both the R&B and country charts. The follow-up "Great Balls of Fire" was an even bigger hit, featuring in the film *Jamboree* and topping the chart across the pond in the UK. A great part of Jerry's appeal was down to his showmanship—he would frequently kick away his piano stool, hammer the keys with his fists and feet, and whirl the mic stand around his head. His private life lived up to this on-stage persona, and his fame began to wane after he attempted to tour the UK with his new wife—who also happened to be his 13-year-old second cousin.

and recordings

Doo Wop
Form of music performed by black vocal groups from the late forties to the late fifties. Characterized by (often unaccompanied) group harmonies, sometimes with falsetto vocal parts.

Suggested listening:

The Ravens	*The Greatest Group of Them All*
The Flamingos	*Doo Bop She Bop: The Best Of*
The Coasters	*Greatest Hits*
The Platters	*The Platters*

Little Richard

One of twelve children, Richard Wayne Penniman was steeped in gospel music throughout his childhood in Macon, Georgia. As well as singing in his local church choir, he would also have been exposed to blues, country, and vaudeville music.

Up until the mid fifties, Little Richard was playing fairly unexceptional jump blues and R&B, but he was still competent enough to win a 1955 recording session at Specialty Records in New Orleans. The session with producer Robert "Bumps" Blackwell was passing uneventfully until Little Richard started messing around during a break with a tune with obscene lyrics. The song's unique style was to set the tone for the rest of Little Richard's career—manic piano playing, falsetto whoops, and nonsense lyrics combined with a driving beat and relentless energy. When the track was released with cleaned-up lyrics under the title "Tutti Frutti," it was a huge R&B and pop hit.

Little Richard, like Jerry Lee Lewis, spiced up his performances with outrageous on-stage behavior—he wore huge baggy suits, huge amounts of stage make-up, and quiffed his hair into enormous and outlandish styles (indeed, Lewis may have been influenced by Little Richard's antics). However, unlike Jerry Lee, he wrote most of his own material, and followed the success of "Tutti Frutti" with a succession of bona fide rock and roll classics like "Long Tall Sally," "Slippin' and Slidin'," "Jenny, Jenny," "Keep a Knockin'," "Good Golly, Miss Molly," and "The Girl Can't Help It," the latter of which featured, along with Little Richard himself, in the rock 'n' roll movie of the same name.

Little Richard's rock 'n' roll career came to an abrupt end in 1957, when he quit in the middle of an Australian tour to enroll at an Alabama bible college. Religion was to keep him out of the public eye for several years, although he eventually returned to performance in the mid sixties after interest was rekindled by new bands like the Rolling Stones and The Beatles (who covered "Long Tall Sally" in 1964).

Chuck Berry

Chuck Berry is probably the single most important figure in the development of rock 'n' roll and possibly the most influential black pop musician ever.

Chuck didn't begin to play guitar professionally until the age of 26, after previous stints as a janitor, photographer, and carpenter. In 1952, after a three-year spell in prison for armed robbery, he joined St. Louis group the Sir John Trio, led by pianist Johnnie Johnson and featuring drummer Eddie Hardy. Johnson's piano playing was to form the backbone of Chuck's sound throughout the fifties and sixties, and indeed, his boogie-woogie inspired piano style became a huge influence on Chuck's guitar playing.

The group quickly became one of the area's top acts and soon secured a residency at the Cosmopolitan Club in the east of the city. Although the band mostly played blues and ballads,

Influential styles

Jump Blues

The dominant form of black music in the late forties. Developed from the big swing bands of the thirties (Count Basie, Cab Calloway, Lionel Hampton, etc.) but really came into vogue after World War II, when Louis Jordan enjoyed huge success.

Suggested listening:

Joe Liggins & His Honeydrippers	*Joe Liggins & The Honeydrippers*
Roy Milton & His Solid Senders	*Roy Milton & His Solid Senders*
Camille Howard	*Vol. 1: Rock Me Daddy*
Amos Milburn	*Blues, Barrelhouse & Boogie: The Best Of, 1946-1955*

they noticed that the local crowd responded best to hillbilly tunes. Chuck began performing his versions of hillbilly songs, and, before long, white fans were turning up in droves to hear him.

In 1955, Chuck and Johnnie traveled to Chicago and bumped into bluesman Muddy Waters in a nightclub, who advised them to get in touch with the Chess label. Chuck duly did so, putting forward an original song called "Ida Mae," which was impressive enough to win a recording contract. When released under the title "Maybelline" (featuring Johnnie Johnson on piano and blues legend Willie Dixon on bass) the song was a huge hit, selling over a million copies. Despite the fact that he was nearly 30, Chuck seemed to have an insight into the music that teenagers wanted to hear, and from 1957-60 he produced a string of rock and roll classics including "Roll Over Beethoven," "Brown-Eyed Man," "Sweet Little Sixteen," "Johnny B. Goode," and many other superb tracks.

Buddy Holly

Born on September 7th, 1936, Buddy Holly possessed a love of music that showed itself at an early age, as he learned to play both the violin and the piano; however, it was the guitar that eventually became his favorite instrument, and it was with his beloved acoustic that he made his first recording in 1949 at his home in Lubbock, Texas (a cover of "My Two Timin' Woman," by Hank Snow).

By the age of 13, Buddy was performing at local country clubs, and throughout the early fifties he recorded various tracks with friends, forming the Western and Bop Band, and the Buddy, Bob, and Larry Trio. The fledgling band got their first break when a scout for Decca heard them opening a local show by Bill Haley; after hearing their demos, he was impressed enough to offer Buddy a solo deal. However, recording sessions in Nashville did not go well, and neither Decca nor Buddy was happy with the results. Despite this, Buddy's first single was issued on April 16th 1956, and within a few months "Blue Days, Black Nights" had sold a fairly respectable 19,000 copies.

However, Decca decided that Buddy still wasn't quite what they wanted, and advised him to return home to Lubbock. It was back in his hometown that he opened a show for Elvis Presley, which convinced him that he needed to move from his country roots into a more rock 'n' roll direction. He formed a new band, The Crickets, and in early 1957 they recorded Holly's track "That'll Be The Day" at the New Mexico studio of producer Norman Petty. By the end of the year, the song had reached #1 on the pop charts and #2 on the R&B chart. In spring 1958, he joined a tour billed as "Alan Freed's Big Beat Show," featuring other rock 'n' rollers Chuck Berry and Jerry Lee Lewis.

In a period of just two years, Buddy wrote and recorded songs that have gone on to form part of the rock 'n' roll canon, including "Rave On," "Peggy Sue," "Oh Boy!," and "Maybe Baby." His short career was brought to a tragic and premature end in the winter of 1958, when a plane carrying Buddy, Ritchie Valens, and the Big Bopper (best known for his hit single "Chantilly Lace") crashed in a cornfield outside Mason City, Iowa.

and recordings

Rockabilly

Form of early rock 'n' roll developed in the first half of the fifties, drawing on strains of honky-tonk and hillbilly boogie. Most famously heard in recordings on the Sun label by Carl Perkins, Elvis Presley, and Jerry Lee Lewis

Suggested listening:

Sonny Burgess	*We Wanna Boogie*
Roy Orbison	*The Sun Years*
Charlie Rich	*The Sun Sessions*
Various	*The Sun Story*

Fats Domino

Antoine "Fats" Domino was born on February 26th 1928, in New Orleans, and learned piano as a child from his brother-in-law. After leaving school, Fats got a job as a factory worker, but he supplemented his income by playing in local clubs like the Hideaway, where he was heard in 1949 by bandleader Dave Bartholomew and Lew Chudd of Imperial Records. Bartholomew was to co-write many Fats Domino tracks over the next 20 years, and their partnership started with the Top 10 R&B hit "The Fat Man" (yet another candidate for "first rock 'n' roll record").

In the early fifties, Fats Domino's profile grew as he toured the country, having R&B hits with songs like "Goin' Home," "Going to the River," "Please Don't Leave Me," and "Don't You Know." Fats went on to sell more records than any other black artist in the fifties, after white teenagers, hungry for rock 'n' roll, discovered him in 1955. His first crossover success came with "Ain't That a Shame," but it wasn't until "I'm In Love Again" was released that he had a Top 10 pop hit.

His next big success, "Blueberry Hill," was inspired by Louis Armstrong's 1949 version but went on to become the song that, for many, defined the Fats Domino sound. Fats's playing was inspired by boogie woogie pianists like Albert Ammons, Meade Lux Lewis, and Little Willie Littlefield, whose techniques he blended with Cajun, blues, and even Latin influences to create his own unique and laid-back style. Indeed, in the frenetic days of early rock 'n' roll, Fats's performances were often considered a little too relaxed, and several of his singles were speeded up after recording to inject a little more pace.

Pioneer record labels

Atlantic

Formed in 1947 in New York, became the most important R&B label of the fifties. Signed Jerry Lieber and Mike Stoller as an independent songwriting team in 1956.

Acts included:

The Drifters	Ray Charles
The Coasters	Big Joe Turner

Chess

Originally formed as Aristocrat Records in Chicago in 1947 by the Chess brothers, Leonard and Phil. Became Chess records in 1949 and was associated with blues throughout the fifties. Willie Dixon became their in-house songwriter in 1952.

Acts included:

Muddy Waters	Elmore James
Howlin' Wolf	Chuck Berry
John Lee Hooker	Bo Diddley

Sun

Established in 1953 in Memphis by Sam Phillips. Made early recordings of Elvis Presley before becoming established as the main rockabilly label later in the decade.

Acts included:

Elvis Presley	Johnny Cash
Carl Perkins	Roy Orbison

Rock 'n' Roll on the World Wide Web

There's a wealth of rock 'n' roll material available for free on the Internet, so if you want to find out more, why not check out some of these sites:

www.rockhall.com

The official website of the Rock and Roll Hall of Fame. Interesting biographies of inductees from all periods of rock history, plus information about exhibits at the museum.

www.history-of-rock.com

Fascinating site covering the years 1954-1963, which attempts to uncover the musical and cultural forces that combined to create rock 'n' roll.

www.rhythmandtheblues.org.uk

Comprehensive site devoted to R&B, complete with extensive section on blues and R&B history.

www.rocknrollvault.com

Packed with interesting rock 'n' roll facts, and includes a timeline of rock.

www.allmusic.com

One of the most comprehensive databases of information on popular music on the Web. Includes extensive biographies and discographies as well as music maps tracing the evolution of musical styles.

www.rocksbackpages.com

Bills itself as the "online library of rock and roll" and features classic articles by rock journalists dating back to the early sixties.

www.tsimon.com

Extensive set of biographies of bands, solo acts, songs, record producers, songwriters, and DJ's from the fifties and sixties.

www.oldiesmusic.com

Huge collection of information for fans of fifties and sixties music, including their own record and book stores.

www.rocklibrary.com

Website of a non-profit organization working to build the world's largest music information archive. Still under construction at time of publication.

www.rocknrollzone.com

Website covering all things rock and roll—includes two online radio stations.

www.hoyhoy.com

Absorbing site dealing with rock and roll music pre-Elvis, focusing on the hard rocking sax-based R&B of the period 1949 to 1953.

www.fiftiesweb.com

Site celebrating fifties culture and the baby boomer generation. Covers everything from TV shows to fashion and popular slang of the time.

Part Two

ROCK 'N' ROLL TECHNIQUES

How to Approach Rock 'n' Roll Piano—A Guide for the Classically Trained Pianist

Those readers who've been through a formal music education may find some of what follows contradictory to standard practice (i.e., what your piano teacher taught you). If so, don't worry. This is rock 'n' roll—it's supposed to be rebellious!

In fact, when playing rock 'n' roll piano, you can throw away the rulebook on technique, because just about anything goes. Want to use your elbow to bash out some chord clusters? Go ahead! Use your feet to reach those tricky bass notes? No sweat!

Just remember that most famous rock 'n' roll players were self-taught; they didn't have a piano teacher telling them the right or wrong way to play. They just played the way that seemed natural to them and made a sound that they liked. And that's exactly the approach you should try, because it's the only way to develop your own individual style.

In fact, a "classical" piano technique may actually stop you from getting the percussive power that you need for a truly electrifying rock 'n' roll performance. That's not to say that you can't still play all your classical favorites—you just need a different mindset to play Little Richard than Debussy.

Practice Tips

Having said the above, some advice that classical piano players follow will also apply to rock 'n' rollers, and one of those is to *practice*—if you really want to improve as a rock 'n' roll piano player, you're going to have to put in some hours of hard work.

The key to rock 'n' roll piano technique is total security in the left hand—you need to be able to play those 12-bar patterns on auto-pilot; then you can concentrate on what your right hand is up to.

So, start by isolating the left hand, and concentrate on two elements:

- **Fingering:** Come up with a fingering that works for you, and stick with it. Don't allow yourself to just use ad-hoc fingerings that change every time you play a pattern.

- **Rhythm:** Your left-hand rhythm has to be rock-solid. Practice the left-hand pattern very slowly and deliberately, and then gradually speed up. If you try to play at top speed from the very beginning, you will never be able to create a solid rhythmic base.

If you're playing with a band, listen to the bass player and drummer (otherwise known as the *rhythm section)*. Try to "lock in" your left hand with the bass player and the bass drum (in fact, you may well find that your left hand is doubling the bass guitar part exactly).

Only once your left hand is totally secure can you then move on to the "more exciting stuff" in the right hand!

Little and Often

The only way that you're going to be able to build up strength and stamina is by practicing little and often. Just like an athlete preparing for a big race, you need to build your musical fitness up over a long period of time. Not only that, but your brain takes time to learn new skills—*muscle memory* (the ability of your hands to find their way around the keyboard without too much attention from your brain) is based on repetition, reinforced by intelligent practice.

A Practice Plan

A thirty-minute practice session could be broken up as follows:

First ten minutes: Warm up.

- Practice scales with left and right hands, separately and together.
- Practice the blues scale in different keys, concentrating on non-pianistic keys like E and A major that are favored by bands.
- Practice left-hand arpeggios and broken chords, in as many different keys as possible.
- Give your left hand a comprehensive workout with a succession of left-hand boogie woogie patterns.

Second ten minutes: Isolate difficult sections.

- Look at a particular tune that you're having difficulty with, and identify the sections where you constantly trip up—this may be just a short section of a bar or less. Don't waste time playing through the 95% of a tune that you know you can do; it's much more effective to concentrate on the 5% that you can't!
- Isolate the section, and try to figure out what's causing the problem—is it a fingering issue? A rhythmic difficulty?
- Slow the section down, almost to a crawl, and practice each hand separately, aiming always to maintain a precise rhythm.
- Once each hand is totally secure, put hands together and then gradually bring up to speed.

Third ten minutes: Cut loose!

- Just have fun, and blast through your favorite tune.
- Try improvising a new solo or play along with one of your favorite records.

If you can find the self-discipline to do this every day, you'll start to see a very real improvement in a matter of weeks. And remember that, although practicing may not seem cool (or very rock 'n' roll), everyone has to do it!

The Left Hand

The key to a successful rock 'n' roll piano technique lies in a powerful, rhythmic, and totally secure left hand. This is the bedrock over which all the "fun stuff" in the right hand is built. Let's start by examining some classic boogie woogie left-hand patterns.

Pattern No. 1

This distinctive 12/8 or shuffle rhythm is characteristic of boogie woogie, and therefore is also commonly found in rock 'n' roll. Emphasize the downbeats (**1**-&-a, **2**-&-a, **3**-&-a, **4**-&-a), and lighten the upbeats—this will make it easier to maintain a "rock steady" beat. Find a fingering that works for you and stick with it, and try to keep your wrist loose at all times.

Listen to the demonstration recording on Track 1, and then play along with the backing on Track 2.

TRACK 1
Demo

TRACK 2
Backing Track

Pattern No. 2

TRACK 3
Demo

TRACK 4
Backing Track

This classic shuffle pattern has been used countless times and gives a fuller, meatier sound. Once again, the trick to keeping the pattern moving is to lighten the upbeat eighth notes. Concentrate on keeping the rhythm even and steady.

Pattern No. 3

TRACK 5
Demo

TRACK 6
Backing Track

Finally, try this slightly more complex pattern, another standard boogie woogie bass line. There's really only one fingering that works for this—just make sure that you use your fourth finger on the E, and you should be OK.

Keep practicing all three patterns until you can play them all with your eyes closed; they need to become so automatic that you don't even need to think about what you're doing.

All these patterns have the same basic function; they outline the chord in a rhythmic and characteristic pattern that can then be moved (and adapted if necessary) for each chord in a progression. Let's now try and apply these basic patterns to a classic rock 'n' roll chord sequence.

Basic Chord Sequences

Here's the good news: Virtually every rock 'n' roll song in the world can be played with just three chords (and some need even fewer). This makes life easier for all concerned and means that if you turn up at a rock 'n' roll gig and don't know the tunes, you've got a pretty good chance of guessing what the chord sequence is going to be.

The three chords in question are built on the 1st, 4th, and 5th degrees of the scale (otherwise known as the *tonic, subdominant,* and *dominant*). In the key of C, they would be the chords C, F, and G respectively; in the key of G, they would be the chords G, C, and D.

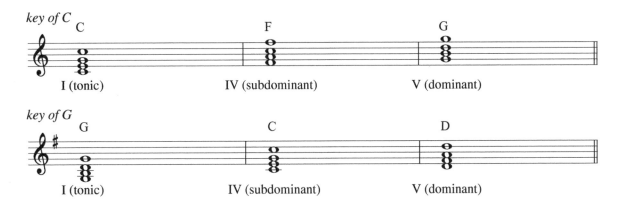

Sometimes, rock 'n' rollers spice these chords up by adding the flattened seventh to form chords known as *dominant sevenths,* or just plain "7ths" for short.

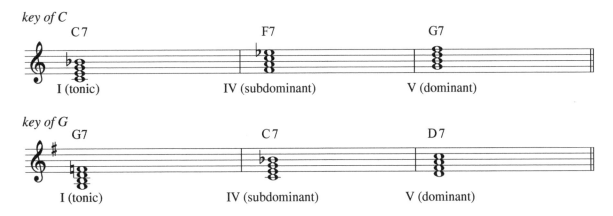

The classic rock 'n' roll sequence is known as a *12-bar* and uses these three chords in the following order:

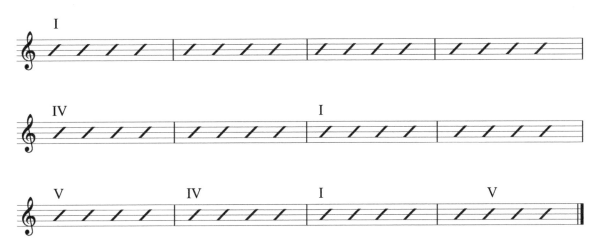

Let's take one of the left-hand patterns and apply it to the 12-bar sequence:

Notice how the basic pattern is simply moved to the fourth and fifth degrees of the scale for the relevant bars. Practice this progression until you are absolutely secure, and, if possible, transpose to other keys such as E, A, and D. Focus particularly on the transition between chords, and make sure that you really hit the first note of the pattern in those bars.

Guitarists, Keys, and Other Necessities

Q: How do you shut up a guitarist?

A: Put some sheet music in front of him.

While this old joke is undoubtedly based on truth, one other way of getting the rock 'n' roll guitarist to shut up is to ask him to play in E♭ major, because chances are he won't be able to.

Guitarists are creatures of habit, and, generally speaking, they only like to play in three keys: E, A, or D. This is because those are the bottom three strings of the guitar, and they provide essential reference points for most guitarists. If he's playing in one of these three keys, then the guitarist can use a selection of easier open chord shapes and a whole host of rock 'n' roll licks that use open strings.

So, in a band setting, you'd better get used to the idea that you're going to be asked to play in these three keys. It's no good just practicing your chops in C, F, and G, because when you get to the rehearsal, you're going to have to do some quick transposition!

Interestingly, if you look at tunes written by great rock 'n' roll pianists like Little Richard, they tend to be in piano-friendly keys like C and G, whereas Chuck Berry tunes are more often in E and A. And of course, if you're going to be playing with a horn section, then you might end up jamming in B♭ or E♭!

Now try the other two patterns, applied to the same chord sequence:

Rock 'n' Roll Tip—The Turnaround

Bar 12 of a 12-bar is known as the *turnaround* because it literally turns the sequence around and gets you back to chord I for the start of the next twelve bars, when the form repeats.

Usually, this turnaround consists of a V chord (which resolves nicely to the I chord when the 12-bar starts again), but sometimes, the turnaround just remains on the tonic (I) chord.

In more harmonically advanced rock 'n' roll tunes (and in a lot of jazz standards), the chords in the turnaround are replaced with more harmonically exciting chords, which can liven up an otherwise predictable sequence.

TRACK 13
Demo

TRACK 14
Backing Track

Sometimes the 12-bar sequence was shortened to an eight-bar pattern, or other irregular lengths, in order to fit the words of the song. This example in the style of Jerry Lee Lewis uses the same three chords as the 12-bar, but shortens the pattern considerably:

The left-hand pattern mirrors a classic rock 'n' roll guitar riff frequently used by Chuck Berry. Indeed, you'll often find that your left hand is doubling parts played by other instruments in the band—usually the bass and/or sax. Always try to listen for this, and make sure that you lock your left hand in with the other members of the band.

TRACK 15
Demo

TRACK 16
Backing Track

Check out this example, in which the left hand of the piano part is doubled throughout by the tenor sax. Try and hone in on the sax part and play exactly in time:

While these classic high-energy left-hand patterns are common to a great many rock 'n' roll tunes, you can also find more mellow tunes and ballads that have a gentler left-hand style.

TRACK 17
Demo

TRACK 18
Backing Track

Try this classic pattern in the style of Fats Domino, with a chord sequence that's a little more adventurous than a standard 12-bar.

Notice how the basic left-hand pattern is adapted in bars 10 and 13 to fit the more unusual chords in this sequence, and check out the classic Fats Domino ending. Slower rock 'n' roll tunes and ballads were much more likely to stray from the tried and trusted three-chord formula of the 12-bar, and often used more sophisticated chord types such as minor sevenths.

By now you should be building up strength, stamina, and dexterity in your left hand. As you move on and start playing the more flashy and exciting right-hand parts, it's easy to neglect your left hand, so it's a good idea to start any practice session by giving your left hand a good workout on some of these patterns.

The Right Hand

In rock 'n' roll, the right hand has two main functions:

* To propel the song forward through driving rhythmic patterns

* To make the part more interesting through embellishing licks and phrases, effects, and general showmanship!

In the fifties and early sixties, piano solos were rare on rock 'n' roll records, with the solo instrument of choice more likely to be a saxophone, so an important secondary role for the pianist was to be able to accompany the soloist in a sensitive manner.

Rock 'n' Roll Eighths

One of the most enduring images of the rock 'n' roll era has to be Jerry Lee Lewis hammering out those frenetic right-hand chords at the top of the keyboard. Jerry knew that this simple technique was guaranteed to inject huge amounts of energy and excitement into any song, and indeed, his right-hand parts frequently consisted of little else.

TRACK 19
Demo
(slow)

TRACK 20
Backing Track
(slow)

Try this simple sequence, which combines a classic left-hand pattern that you've come across already, with repeated eighth notes high in the right hand—you've paid for those dusty keys at the top of the keyboard, so why not use them!

You can really hammer the eighth notes, but be careful not to let your wrist lock up, as this will prevent you from playing these patterns at high speed, as well as potentially damaging your hand and wrist. Most of the action should come from the wrist and not from your arm.

Once you're happy at a slower tempo, try speeding things up a bit:

TRACK 21
Demo
(full speed)

TRACK 22
Backing Track
(full speed)

When rehearsing any of the examples in this section, remember to isolate the left-hand part first and make sure that it is totally secure, before adding the right-hand part. As the right-hand parts become more syncopated, you'll find that they start to interfere with the left-hand rhythm, so aim for complete independence between the hands right from the start.

Try this example, in which the right hand echoes the left-hand pattern, while still providing a powerful motor rhythm:

TRACK 23
Demo
(slow)

TRACK 24
Backing Track
(slow)

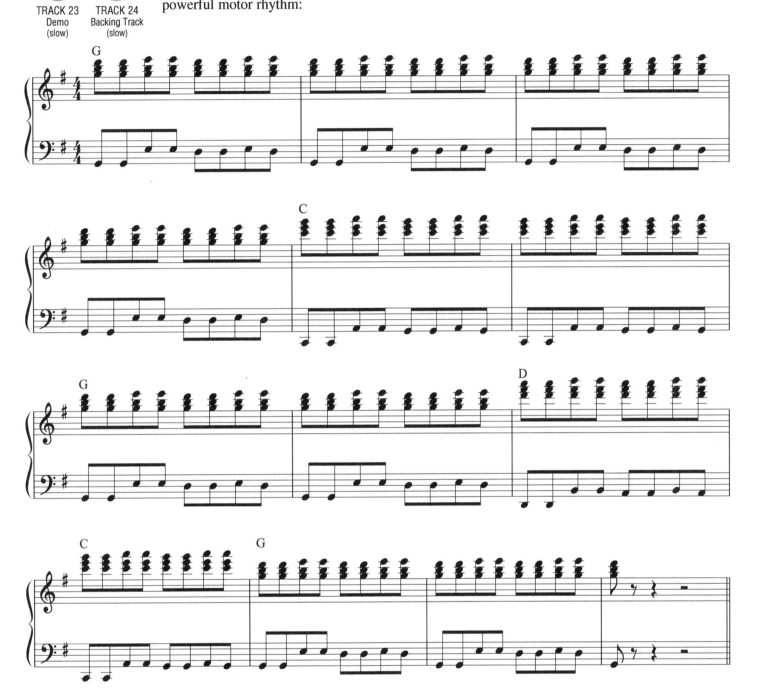

Once you're happy at the slower tempo, try this faster version:

TRACK 25
Demo
(full speed)

TRACK 26
Backing Track
(full speed)

Straight Eighths vs. Swung Eighths

TRACK 27
Demo

TRACK 28
Backing Track

In the examples you've just played, the eighth notes are even, or *straight*. However, if the song is *swung*, each beat is divided into three eighth notes instead of two, and so the right hand plays triplets, as in this Fats Domino-style sequence:

Rock 'n' Roll Tip—Straight No Chaser

Famous rock 'n' roll pianists like Little Richard frequently played somewhere in between straight and swung eighths, but this is not recommended for the novice rock 'n' roller!

It is possible to combine straight and triplet eighths in the same tune. Check out this example, which starts with straight eighths and then moves up a gear into triplets.

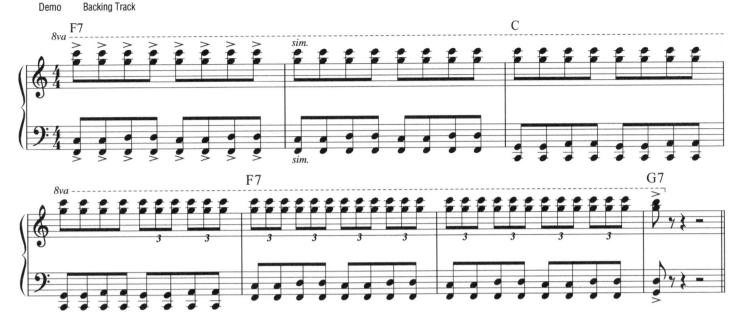

Don't worry too much about the timing of the triplet figures—just make sure that the first one of each group hits the beat, and the others will look after themselves. Remember to keep your wrist relaxed; if you lock your wrist, you'll never be able to get up to speed. If necessary, during practice, play quarter notes in the bass until you've got the sound of the triplets clear in your head—then put the eighth notes back in. The clash of the two rhythms is part of the appeal, so persevere until you can do it without thinking! (In fact, if you listen closely to the recordings of Jerry Lee Lewis, his left hand sometimes drops back to quarter notes in sections like this.)

The advanced rock 'n' roller might even want to increase the speed of the right-hand pattern further, into sixteenth notes, as in this example:

Notice that the chord shape used in the right hand over the C chord. It's actually a C7#9, which combines both the major and minor third of the chord, for a delicious tension and crunchiness. Major/minor ambiguity is a key characteristic of rock 'n' roll, boogie woogie, and particularly blues.

ROCK 'N' ROLL TECHNIQUES NO. 1
The Glissando

The *glissando* is a classic rock 'n' roll device that's been used on hundreds of great tunes. In fact, it's probably one of the simplest and most satisfying sounds that you can get out of a piano. It's used so frequently in rock 'n' roll that you're going to need to get your technique sorted out; otherwise, you'll cut your fingers to ribbons.

The key to pain-free glissandos is to use your nails rather than the pads of your fingers. There are two basic options:

1. Bend the thumb of your right hand under the other fingers, and drag across the white keys. This technique is best used when glissing from the top of the keyboard down towards the bottom.

2. Turn your right hand over so that the palm is facing upwards, and use the nails of all four fingers. This is the most convenient method to use when glissing upwards, although it can also be used in the opposite direction.

Practice both options in both directions, and decide which one is most comfortable for you—most rock 'n' roll pianists use a combination of both. Since your left hand is going to be occupied for the most part with maintaining its boogie patterns, focus most of your attention on practicing right-hand glisses.

Once you feel comfortable with your gliss technique, try this exercise, which combines glisses with eighth-note patterns. You need to be fast and accurate with your glisses in order to get your hand in position to play the eighth notes. When playing a downward gliss, be sure to leave enough time to get your hand back up to the top of the keyboard to continue the eighth-note patterns.

TRACK 33
Demo

TRACK 34
Backing Track

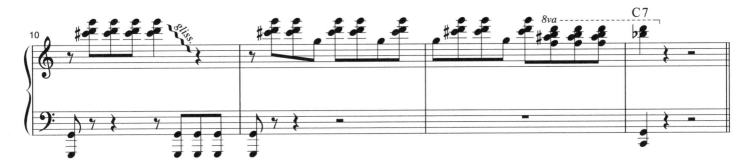

Think carefully about how you're going to finger the right-hand chord that comes immediately before any downward gliss. Wherever possible, you need to play the bottom white note of that chord with your thumb, so that when the time comes for the downward gliss, you can just drag your hand from right to left. So, for example, in bar 2, the final quarter note of the bar should be played with a thumb on the G, and your fifth finger on the C. Similarly, the crunchy chord in bars 8-10, should be played with your second finger on the C♯, your thumb on the D, and your little finger on the G.

The triplet run in bars 7-8 was a favorite of Jerry Lee Lewis, and is actually a lot easier than it looks. The run can be broken down into two triplet groups beginning on B♭ and F respectively, both of which can be played with the first three fingers only.

This is a challenging example, so practice slowly, hands separately, and make sure that you've worked out all your fingering in advance, before you attempt to play hands together.

Use of the Pedal

There are several very good reasons why rock 'n' roll piano players don't use the pedal very much, if it all.

- Firstly, the main element of the rock 'n' roll sound is the percussive driving force that you can get by really pounding a piano keyboard. Use of the pedal will just blur those percussive eighth notes into a foggy mess.

- Secondly, rock 'n' roll pianists have better things to do with their feet, like thumping out the beat, or smashing the top end of the keyboard.

- And finally of course, it's very difficult to use the pedal if you're standing up!

However, one time you do need to use the pedal is when playing glisses—jam the pedal down at the start of the gliss and hold it down until you've reached the bottom (or top) to create a fantastic wash of sound.

ROCK 'N' ROLL TECHNIQUES NO. 2
Crushed Notes

The relationship between rock 'n' roll piano playing and rock 'n' roll guitar playing is a close one—for example, Chuck Berry was heavily influenced by his piano player Johnnie Johnson, while many licks and accompaniment patterns are common to both instruments.

However, there are some things that you can do on a guitar that simply can't be done on the piano. One such technique is known as *string bending,* where the guitarist bends the string with his fretting hand, causing the pitch of the note to rise.

Because the piano can only play discrete pitches (it can play F or F♯, but it can't play any of the microtones in between), it's impossible to accurately reproduce this effect. However, with a little bit of ingenuity, the rock 'n' roll pianist can get close—by literally crushing in an extra (very short) note. Over time, this has become an accepted part of the rock 'n' roll sound in its own right, and is an essential part of any rock 'n' roll pianist's repertoire of techniques.

TRACK 35
Demo

TRACK 36
Backing Track

In this example, a C♯ is crushed in front of a bar of eighth notes. Although the notation shows that the crushed note appears before the D and G notes, in practice, the C♯ and G are played at the same time, with the C♯ sliding swiftly to the D.

Practice the right hand without the crushed note using your second and fifth fingers for the D and G notes, respectively. Then, practice hitting C♯ and G together with the same two fingers, sliding your second finger from C♯ to D as quickly as possible. Finally, put the two elements together and practice along with Track 36.

TRACK 37
Demo

TRACK 38
Backing Track

Now try this example, which includes two crushed notes per bar:

26

TRACK 39
Demo

TRACK 40
Backing Track

The crushed note is also an essential component of boogie woogie piano playing, as this example shows:

The Roll

A key characteristic of the piano is that, once you have hit a note, it begins to die away (unlike the organ, for example, where the volume of the note will continue at a constant level for as long as the key is pressed down).

Given that one of the defining features of rock 'n' roll is volume, this could pose a problem for an aspiring rock 'n' roll pianist, especially if you have to compete with drums and electric guitars. Of course, one very effective way of maintaining volume and energy is to use straight or swung eighths, as we've already seen.

Another option is to use the *roll*—a tremolo effect formed by rocking the hand rapidly from side to side.

Try this version of the previous example, which has rolls added to the longer notes:

TRACK 41　　TRACK 42
Demo　　Backing Track

You should find the two-note rolls fairly straightforward—as ever, the key is to keep your wrist loose and relaxed. The three-note roll in the last bar of this example is a little more challenging: The trick here is to divide the three notes into two groups (either the top two notes together and the bottom one separate, or vice versa) and then just alternate rapidly between them.

The same principle can be applied to four-note chords that are rolled; in this example, the four-note chord in bar 4 can be divided into two parts—the top three notes together and the bottom note—which can then be alternated with one another.

TRACK 43
Demo

TRACK 44
Backing Track

The Note Cluster

A large part of rock 'n' roll piano playing is to do with generating sound effects rather than specific musical phrases and licks. When you're hammering away at the top end of the keyboard, it actually doesn't really matter what notes you're playing—what's important is, firstly, that you're generating high frequency sound that can be heard above the drums, bass, and horn section, and secondly, that the audience can see that you're a wild man (or woman) of rock, who has clearly sold a soul to the Devil in return for outstanding piano playing abilities.

Manic rock 'n' roll pianists like Little Richard and Jerry Lee Lewis would use all sorts of unconventional methods to get effects out of their piano, including using their fists, elbows, and feet to smash out *note clusters* at both ends of the keyboard.

In fact, for the canny rock 'n' roller, the note cluster offers a neat way out of improvisational difficulties. Having a problem figuring out how to end that solo? No problem, just bash out a descending pattern with your fists, as shown in this continuation of the previous example:

TRACK 45
Demo

TRACK 46
Backing Track

While you may want to cultivate the air of a rock 'n' roll maniac who would use just about any part of their body to abuse a piano, it's wise to take some precautions to prevent damage to your hands (or your piano). Your instinct might be to clench your fist and then use the bottom end, near your little finger, to bash the keyboard, but it's actually less painful to rotate your hand 90 degrees and use your knuckles. This method also has the advantage that when you want to return to more traditional styles of playing, your hand is already in the right position, and all you need to do is unclench your fist.

Elbows and legs are less easy to control, and you run a much greater risk of damaging your piano, but if you are supple enough to get your legs up onto the keyboard, then go for it!

All the World's a Stage...

Although players like Little Richard and Jerry Lee Lewis were great rock 'n' roll pianists, they both realized early in their careers that above all they had to be great showmen.

Sure, brilliant piano playing was part of the attraction, and great songs helped too, but what really made them international stars were their crazy stage antics. So, even if your piano playing's not up to their standard, there are plenty of other tips you can pick up from these great entertainers.

First up, why not dress up to go on stage? Lurid, brightly colored suits with huge baggy pants always go down well, perhaps teamed with a pair of leopard-skin "brothel-creepers." Clashing fluorescent colors and lots of glitter will really make you stand out on stage.

Why not grow your hair and then backcomb and gel it into a huge pompadour that towers precariously above your head? (Or alternatively, just get a wig.) And don't hold back on the stage make up, either.

And once you get to the piano, there's a wealth of moves to employ. Bash out notes with your fist, elbows, feet or even your head, kick away the piano stool at strategic moments, and lean backwards and forwards at random intervals, and you should soon have the audience in a frenzy.

Comping

Amid all this talk of showmanship and outrageous piano techniques, it's easy to forget that in a rock 'n' roll band the piano's main role is to accompany and support either the singer or other solo instruments. In fact, for classically trained pianists, it may come as a shock to have to think of the piano as anything other than a solo instrument. But in a rock 'n' roll band, you will find that for long stretches of time all you will need to do is outline the chord sequence, leaving room for the other members of the band to do their thing.

This basic chordal playing is known as *comping* (from "accompanying") and is an essential technique for any rock 'n' roll pianist. It's vital to develop a sense of when to sit back in the band and let other players step forward. If you can do this, you'll get respect from your colleagues—and they'll be more likely to support you when it's your turn in the limelight.

TRACK 47
Demo

TRACK 48
Backing Track

Look at this example, in a Buddy Holly style. The tenor sax is carrying the tune, so all you need to do is sit back, keep the left hand precise, and add off-beat chord stabs in the right hand:

In contrast to solo sections, where you can use the full range of the keyboard, when comping it's advisable to restrict yourself to the middle octaves. This will prevent your sound from interfering with the soloist, and you'll blend in with the band much better.

TRACK 49
Demo

TRACK 50
Backing Track

Here's another example featuring a tenor sax solo. Keep the left hand rhythmic, and place the right-hand chord stabs lightly but accurately. If you're in any doubt about where the chords go, listen to the trumpet part and try to match its offbeat entries with your right hand.

TRACK 51
Demo

TRACK 52
Backing Track

It's hard enough keeping guitarists quiet at the best of times, so when they're taking a solo it's best not to get in the way. Check out the following example, and note how the piano comps sensitively. The sax part doubles your chord stabs, so try and lock in your right hand with it.

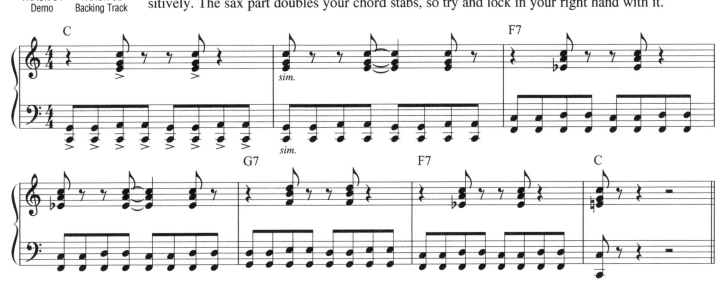

Soloing

Piano solos are actually relatively rare in early rock 'n' roll, but you'll undoubtedly want to play one at some point, and if you're in a gigging band it will be your opportunity to hog the limelight.

TRACK 53
Demo

The Blues Scale

The raw material for almost every rock 'n' roll piano solo is the *blues scale.* Here it is in C:

Pay special attention to the F♯ in this scale, which is also known as the *flattened fifth,* or, by bluesmen, as a *blue note.* It's this note that gives the scale its characteristically dirty sound and bluesy flavor.

You're going to need to know this particular scale inside out, so practice it thoroughly in all keys. It's also a good idea to practice it starting on different notes—for example, you could start a C blues scale on F or G. It's also important to practice the scale ascending and descending. Gradually, your hand will become drawn to certain groupings of notes within the scale, and you'll soon discover some classic rock 'n' roll patterns. Look out for some choice licks in the songs at the end of this book.

How to Construct a Solo

TRACK 54
Demo

TRACK 55
Backing Track

Check out this solo, and pay special attention to how the blues scale is used.

The example is in G and follows the 12-bar pattern—apart from a cheeky extra half bar before the change to C (a common occurrence in early rock 'n' roll, often added because the singer had too many lyrics to fit in!). The first four bars use the G blues scale, switching to the C blues scale over the C chord and reverting to the G blues scale as the chord changes back to G. A triplet figure based on the D7 chord follows before another bar of the C blues scale takes us back to the key chord for another two bars of the G blues scale.

In a 12-bar progression like this, it is actually possible to use the root blues scale (in this example, the blues scale on G) for nearly the whole progression. The only chord that it won't sound good over is the V chord (in this example, D7), and for that bar you will either have to shift to the blues scale on D, or, as in this example, switch to a chordal approach.

Don't Fear the Cliché

Take the time to listen to your favorite players and try to pick up some of their licks and phrases. This is a time-honored principle that rock 'n' roll musicians have been using for years. And don't just restrict yourself to piano players; listen to guitarists and sax players too, and see if you can build some of their lines into your own solo playing.

Don't be afraid of cliché—rock 'n' roll isn't necessarily about being original. It's about having a good time, so feel free to steal from the greats.

Harmonizing in Thirds and Sixths

An alternative approach to soloing is to use a more melodic style, harmonizing in either thirds or sixths. If you're going to attempt this, you need to really know your way around the chord sequence, keeping an eye out for any non-diatonic chords that could upset your harmonization.

TRACK 56
Demo

TRACK 57
Backing Track

Look out for the G7 chord in bar 5 of this example—it's not diatonic to the key of F and so requires the B♭ to be changed into B♮.

Intros, Outros & Stop Choruses

Even if there are limited opportunities for extended piano solos in early rock 'n' roll, there is no shortage of smaller windows of opportunity in which the alert pianist can make his or her mark. Introductions and outros are traditionally points in a song in which an instrumentalist, be he a pianist, guitarist, or saxophonist, features strongly. This is particularly true in rock 'n' roll, because the songs often feature sparse introductions with many "stop" sections, where the rest of the band drop out completely. This leaves you with a completely blank space in which to drop some of your tastiest moves.

Check out this introduction in the Jerry Lee Lewis style. The band punctuate the texture at regular intervals, but in between their interjections, there's plenty of opportunity for some dramatic licks, glisses, and crushed notes:

It seems only fair to return the favor when another band member gets a chance to cut loose:

The key with "stop choruses" like this is to remember that they're coming—it's not very cool to steam into a chorus like this only to find that the rest of the band has stopped. Assuming that you've remembered when you're supposed to stop, make your chord stabs really staccato, and place them accurately and in time with the rest of the band.

TRACK 62
Demo

TRACK 63
Backing Track

Here's an example that moves from straight eighths, into triplets, and then into a "stop section":

It's worth isolating the solo phrases and practicing them slowly until you are totally secure—remember that you're on your own and any mistakes will be obvious to all!

Part Three

STYLE FILE

Here's where you get a chance to put all the techniques you've learned into practice. This section of the book includes six rock 'n' roll tunes composed in different styles, which will allow you to see how rock 'n' roll piano techniques work in context.

Just like real songs, these tunes have different sections, which demand different styles of playing, so you'll need to be able to combine confident solo licks and fills (for intros and solos) with sensitive comping (during verse sections, or when accompanying another solo instrument such as a saxophone).

The songs are presented roughly in order of difficulty, with the hardest piece appearing at the end. The last three tunes are presented at two tempos, so you can practice slowly before attempting the full-speed version.

1. Buddy Brilliant

The first track is a tune written in the style of Buddy Holly. Although Buddy is best remembered as a songwriter and guitarist, his later material did feature piano, mostly in a supporting role. In this piece, your role is to support the tenor sax soloist with some sensitive comping, until you get your chance to shine with a melodic solo in sixths. The solo also features some rolls on the longer notes, which can be omitted if necessary. When you get your chance to play the tune, try and pick up on the phrasing that the tenor sax uses.

Keep the left hand rhythmic and accurate throughout, and be sure to place the offbeat right-hand stabs carefully. Look out for the various "stops" throughout the song, and make sure you know where you're supposed to stop and start. Notice also the use of the F6 chord, which gives a mellower feel than the more conventional F7.

Finally, if possible, try to memorize the song and play along without the music in front of you. You're less likely to make mistakes, and, more importantly, it's a lot more rock 'n' roll!

Buddy Brilliant

2. Raspberry Valley

Next up, we have a mellow 12/8 groove in the style of Fats Domino. Once again, the tenor sax is the star of the show here, and your job is to support and provide some forward movement through the triplet eighth notes. Make sure that your left hand locks in with the rhythm section and that the eighth-note triplets are played firmly and evenly.

Look out for the bars in which the right-hand chords give way to octaves, and try to bring those descending figures out. Look out, too, for the interesting *half-diminished chord* (Cm7♭5) towards the end of the middle eight—an advanced harmony that would have been quite unusual in early rock 'n' roll.

TRACK 66
Demo

TRACK 67
Backing Track

Raspberry Valley

3. A Summer Hideaway

This classic 12/8 ballad demonstrates the softer side of rock 'n' roll. Often, songs of this nature were written with dancing in mind; slower, smoochy numbers like this allowed less competent dancers onto the dance floor, as well as those with romantic intentions.

Given the more romantic style of this song, perhaps it's not surprising to find some more mellow chord voicings; Am7sus4 and Cmaj7 certainly wouldn't be found in your average high-tempo rock 'n' roll party tune.

Once again, lock your left hand in with the rhythm section, and keep the right-hand triplets even and light. Look out, too, for the modulation to A major towards the end of the piece. The final chorus repeats four times, so there's an opportunity for you to try out some improvisation if you want.

TRACK 68
Demo

TRACK 69
Backing Track

A Summer Hideaway

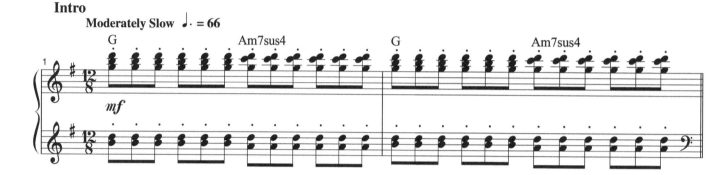

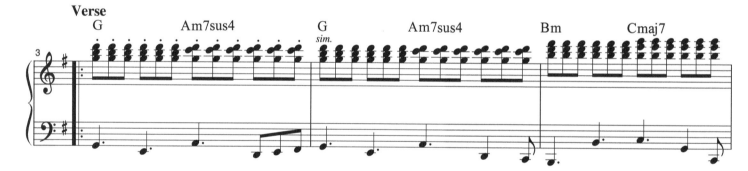

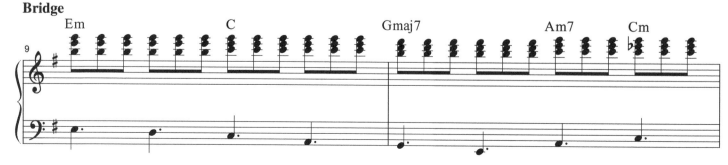

4. Boogie Woogie Wonderland

This funky workout combines various boogie bass lines and left-hand patterns. Try to maintain the rollicking rolling rhythm throughout, keeping the left hand steady as it progresses through the three different patterns. There's plenty of interesting stuff for your right hand here too, with crushed notes, rolls, and passages in thirds to get to grips with. Look out for the triplet figure in bar 23, which cuts across the beat—isolate this bar if necessary and practice very slowly hands together, working out exactly how the left and right hands fit together.

At bar 30, the tenor sax takes a solo—maintain the bass pattern here, and add offbeat chord stabs. If you're feeling ambitious, you could also add a few bluesy licks between the tenor sax phrases. Look out, too, for the classic rock 'n' roll ending, featuring juicy ninth chords!

A slower recording of this track is also included for practice, before you attempt the full-speed version.

  Boogie Woogie Wonderland

TRACK 70
Demo
(slow)

TRACK 71
Backing Track
(slow)

TRACK 72
Demo
(full speed)

TRACK 73
Backing Track
(full speed)

Sax Solo

5. Rick's Rock

This classic 12-bar tune is based on the piano style of Little Richard and is packed full of rock 'n' roll techniques.

The intro starts out with a strident octave opening, with optional rolls, before leading into the first verse with a downward sequence of note clusters that should be played with your fist.

The eighth-note rhythm in this tune is somewhere between swung and even eighths—if in doubt, listen to the tenor sax part, which doubles the left hand. In the more involved right-hand sections, it's possible to reduce the left-hand part to quarter notes, just playing the note that falls on the beat, as the part is doubled throughout. Look out for triplet figures in the right hand, and remember to keep your wrist relaxed and loose when playing them. Try not to think too much about the exact rhythm, and they'll probably come out sounding about right!

This tune also features a couple of 2/4 bars designed to catch the unwary rock 'n' roller off guard! Make sure you know where they are, and count through them carefully. Other sections to look out for are the "stop chorus," the tenor sax solo, and the classic Little Richard ending!

We've also included a slowed down version of this tune to aid your practice.

TRACK 74
Demo
(slow)

TRACK 75
Backing Track
(slow)

Rick's Rock

TRACK 76
Demo
(full speed)

TRACK 77
Backing Track
(full speed)

49

6. Roll Over Jerry!

This high-tempo rocker in the style of Jerry Lee Lewis is a veritable cornucopia of rock 'n' roll techniques, licks, and effects. The classic intro is a great chance for you to shine, but make sure that all your solo licks are totally secure—this is not a good place to make a mistake! The interplay between the right and left hands is crucial; the two parts should really bounce off each other.

There are glissandos all over the place in this tune, so make sure you've got your fingering sorted out before you attempt them. When practicing before a gig, you might want to leave the glisses out to prevent wrecking your hands, and only put them in again when you're really going for it. Jerry's trademark eighths are also in evidence here—look out for the sections where they speed up into triplets, and be sure to keep your wrist and arm relaxed. The same goes for the sixteenth-note phrases towards the end of the song.

This song has more stops and starts than a bus route, so make sure you know where they all are. Look out too for the guitar and tenor sax solos—they provide an ideal opportunity to gather your breath before the next section. The descending runs in bars 51 and 71 are easier than they look. Practice them separately and slowly and work out your fingering carefully, and you should be OK.

Once again, there's a slower version of this track, so don't panic if you can't manage it at full speed!

TRACK 78
Demo
(slow)

TRACK 79
Backing Track
(slow)

Roll Over Jerry!

TRACK 80
Demo
(full speed)

TRACK 81
Backing Track
(full speed)

Verse

KEYBOARD STYLE SERIES

THE COMPLETE GUIDE!

These book/audio packs provide focused lessons that contain valuable how-to insight, essential playing tips, and beneficial information for all players. From comping to soloing, comprehensive treatment is given to each subject. The companion audio features many of the examples in the book performed either solo or with a full band.

BEBOP JAZZ PIANO

by John Valerio

This book provides detailed information for bebop and jazz keyboardists on: chords and voicings, harmony and chord progressions, scales and tonality, common melodic figures and patterns, comping, characteristic tunes, the styles of Bud Powell and Thelonious Monk, and more.

00290535 Book/Online Audio $18.99

BEGINNING ROCK KEYBOARD

by Mark Harrison

This comprehensive book/audio package will teach you the basic skills needed to play beginning rock keyboard. From comping to soloing, you'll learn the theory, the tools, and the techniques used by the pros. The accompanying audio demonstrates most of the music examples in the book.

00311922 Book/Online Audio $14.99

BLUES PIANO

by Mark Harrison

With this book/audio pack, you'll learn the theory, the tools, and even the tricks that the pros use to play the blues. Covers: scales and chords; left-hand patterns; walking bass; endings and turnarounds; right-hand techniques; how to solo with blues scales; crossover licks; and more.

00311007 Book/Online Audio $19.99

BOOGIE-WOOGIE PIANO

by Todd Lowry

From learning the basic chord progressions to inventing your own melodic riffs, you'll learn the theory, tools and techniques used by the genre's best practicioners.

00117067 Book/Online Audio $17.99

BRAZILIAN PIANO

by Robert Willey and Alfredo Cardim

Brazilian Piano teaches elements of some of the most appealing Brazilian musical styles: choro, samba, and bossa nova. It starts with rhythmic training to develop the fundamental groove of Brazilian music.

00311469 Book/Online Audio $19.99

CONTEMPORARY JAZZ PIANO

by Mark Harrison

From comping to soloing, you'll learn the theory, the tools, and the techniques used by the pros. The full band tracks on the audio feature the rhythm section on the left channel and the piano on the right channel, so that you can play along with the band.

00311848 Book/Online Audio $18.99

COUNTRY PIANO

by Mark Harrison

Learn the theory, the tools, and the tricks used by the pros to get that authentic country sound. This book/audio pack covers: scales and chords, walkup and walkdown patterns, comping in traditional and modern country, Nashville "fretted piano" techniques and more.

00311052 Book/Online Audio $19.99

GOSPEL PIANO

by Kurt Cowling

Discover the tools you need to play in a variety of authentic gospel styles, through a study of rhythmic devices, grooves, melodic and harmonic techniques, and formal design. The accompanying audio features over 90 tracks, including piano examples as well as the full gospel band.

00311327 Book/Online Adio $17.99

INTRO TO JAZZ PIANO

by Mark Harrison

From comping to soloing, you'll learn the theory, the tools, and the techniques used by the pros. The accompanying audio demonstrates most of the music examples in the book. The full band tracks feature the rhythm section on the left channel and the piano on the right channel, so that you can play along with the band.

00312088 Book/Online Audio $17.99

JAZZ-BLUES PIANO

by Mark Harrison

This comprehensive book will teach you the basic skills needed to play jazz-blues piano. Topics covered include: scales and chords • harmony and voicings • progressions and comping • melodies and soloing • characteristic stylings.

00311243 Book/Online Audio $17.99

JAZZ-ROCK KEYBOARD

by T. Lavitz

Learn what goes into mixing the power and drive of rock music with the artistic elements of jazz improvisation in this comprehensive book and CD package. This instructional tool delves into scales and modes, and how they can be used with various chord progressions to develop the best in soloing chops.

00290536 Book/CD Pack $17.95

LATIN JAZZ PIANO

by John Valerio

This book is divided into three sections. The first covers Afro-Cuban (Afro-Caribbean) jazz, the second section deals with Brazilian influenced jazz – Bossa Nova and Samba, and the third contains lead sheets of the tunes and instructions for the play-along audio.

00311345 Book/Online Audio $17.99

MODERN POP KEYBOARD

by Mark Harrison

From chordal comping to arpeggios and ostinatos, from grand piano to synth pads, you'll learn the theory, the tools, and the techniques used by the pros. The online audio demonstrates most of the music examples in the book.

00146596 Book/Online Audio $17.99

NEW AGE PIANO

by Todd Lowry

From melodic development to chord progressions to left-hand accompaniment patterns, you'll learn the theory, the tools and the techniques used by the pros. The accompanying 96-track CD demonstrates most of the music examples in the book.

00117322 Book/CD Pack $16.99

POST-BOP JAZZ PIANO

by John Valerio

This book/audio pack will teach you the basic skills needed to play post-bop jazz piano. Learn the theory, the tools, and the tricks used by the pros to play in the style of Bill Evans, Thelonious Monk, Herbie Hancock, McCoy Tyner, Chick Corea and others. Topics covered include: chord voicings, scales and tonality, modality, and more.

00311005 Book/Online Audio $17.99

PROGRESSIVE ROCK KEYBOARD

by Dan Maske

You'll learn how soloing techniques, form, rhythmic and metrical devices, harmony, and counterpoint all come together to make this style of rock the unique and exciting genre it is.

00311307 Book/Online Audio $19.99

R&B KEYBOARD

by Mark Harrison

From soul to funk to disco to pop, you'll learn the theory, the tools, and the tricks used by the pros with this book/audio pack. Topics covered include: scales and chords, harmony and voicings, progressions and comping, rhythmic concepts, characteristic stylings, the development of R&B, and more! Includes seven songs.

00310881 Book/Online Audio $19.99

ROCK KEYBOARD

by Scott Miller

Learn to comp or solo in any of your favorite rock styles. Listen to the audio to hear your parts fit in with the total groove of the band. Includes 99 tracks! Covers: classic rock, pop/rock, blues rock, Southern rock, hard rock, progressive rock, alternative rock and heavy metal.

00310823 Book/Online Audio $17.99

ROCK 'N' ROLL PIANO

by Andy Vinter

Take your place alongside Fats Domino, Jerry Lee Lewis, Little Richard, and other legendary players of the '50s and '60s! This book/audio pack covers: left-hand patterns; basic rock 'n' roll progressions; right-hand techniques; straight eighths vs. swing eighths; glisses, crushed notes, rolls, note clusters and more. Includes six complete tunes.

00310912 Book/Online Audio $18.99

SALSA PIANO

by Hector Martignon

From traditional Cuban music to the more modern Puerto Rican and New York styles, you'll learn the all-important rhythmic patterns of salsa and how to apply them to the piano. The book provides historical, geographical and cultural background info, and the 50+-tracks includes piano examples and a full salsa band percussion section.

00311049 Book/Online Audio $19.99

SMOOTH JAZZ PIANO

by Mark Harrison

Learn the skills you need to play smooth jazz piano – the theory, the tools, and the tricks used by the pros. Topics covered include: scales and chords; harmony and voicings; progressions and comping; rhythmic concepts; melodies and soloing; characteristic stylings; discussions on jazz evolution.

00311095 Book/Online Audio $19.99

STRIDE & SWING PIANO

by John Valerio

Learn the styles of the stride and swing piano masters, such as Scott Joplin, Jimmy Yancey, Pete Johnson, Jelly Roll Morton, James P. Johnson, Fats Waller, Teddy Wilson, and Art Tatum. This book/audio pack covers classic ragtime, early blues and boogie woogie, New Orleans jazz and more. Includes 14 songs.

00310882 Book/Online Audio $19.99

WORSHIP PIANO

by Bob Kauflin

From chord inversions to color tones, from rhythmic patterns to the Nashville Numbering System, you'll learn the tools and techniques needed to play piano or keyboard in a modern worship setting.

00311425 Book/Online Audio $17.99

HAL•LEONARD®

Prices, contents, and availability
subject to change without notice.

www.halleonard.com